MW00980765

Shoto-Kan Karate

The Ultimate in Self-Defense

SHOTO-KAN

Peter Ventresca

KARATE

The Ultimate in
Self-Defense

Published by the Charles E. Tuttle Company, Inc.
of Rutland, Vermont & Tokyo, Japan
with editorial offices at
2-6 Suido 1-chome, Bunkyo-ku, Tokyo 112

© 1970 by Charles E. Tuttle Co., Inc.

LCC Card No. 71-104205
ISBN 0-8048-1658-1

First edition, 1970
First paperback edition, 1990
Fourth printing, 1993

Printed in Japan

To the memory of all Karate Masters:

who, through their patience, wisdom, and understanding in the teaching of Karate, have made it possible for the art to continue to the present day.

EXPLANATION OF THE EMBLEM

Pure white background with the red circle
SYMBOL: The Japanese Flag

The gate
SYMBOL: Serenity

The black belt on the white background
SYMBOL: A reminder of the beginning of
the study of Karate to the stage
of black belt. The end is the
beginning and the study has just
begun.

He who claims to know all is a fool,
for his learning has ceased.
He who knows naught and knows he knows
naught is the enlightened one,
for his wisdom will be great.

CONFUCIUS

Table of Contents

Foreword

There are many books on karate today, and what they generally contain is a maze of pictures showing dramatic and spectacular techniques. Where the techniques come from is very rarely explained. All techniques in karate are contained in the *kata,* or forms.

This book is, I feel, unique, for there has never been one written on such advanced kata as those contained here and, more important, their proper application. In understanding this book, it is essential for the reader to bear in mind that the kata is on the left-hand page executed by one model. The actual application of the same technique is on the opposite page executed by two models. Thus a person wishing to study this book in earnest will be able to see at a glance the techniques of the kata and their proper application.

The purpose of this is to show the effectiveness of karate through the study of the various forms and their application as they were intended. The book specializes primarily on two kata, the presentations of which, it is hoped, will enable the average person to see and understand what actually takes place in an attack.

The kata, Bassai No. 1 and Tekki No. 1, contain advanced movements which, with enough practice, anyone can learn and properly apply. I wish to show that the study of karate can be a very satisfying and rewarding experience without fear of injury to one's self or his partner, by the control of every physical movement made by either party.

I wish to acknowledge my thanks to Frank Cronin for posing for the photographs; to Ralph Moxcey for his skill and patience in taking the pictures, and to Anne Ventresca for the tremendous amount of typing performed to complete this book.

Ralph Moxcey

Peter Ventresca
CHIEF INSTRUCTOR
Shoto-Kan Karate Association of Massachusetts
Headquarters—Ventresca Studio of Japanese Karate,
Boston, Mass.

Introduction

Karate is the defense of one's self from an attack without the aid of any weapon, such as a club, knife, or gun. It is the use of one's own body in a perfectly controlled and precise manner performing highly skilled and intricate movements in a moment of an attack by one or more persons.

The literal meaning of the word "karate" is empty hand or open hand. A person extending a hand in a clenched fist signifies violence (or the past or present performance of a violent act). A person extending the same hand, open, signifies a definite sign of friendliness (as in the shaking of hands). If the need arises, the same open hand can become a violent and devastating instrument of self-defense.

Karate originated in India, and was introduced into China 3,000 years ago. Through a period of time, as it was taught to the people, karate spread north, south, east, and west. Techniques depended upon the locality of its study—if the people studying karate were tall, they specialized in leg techniques; if on the other hand they were short, the specialization was in hand techniques. Thus there are many theories as to the correct movements in karate.

The techniques of karate are called *kata* in Japanese. A kata consists of a number of offensive and defensive techniques with a minimum of twenty movements, with each kata more advanced than the last. Generally these kata are in a form of a style named after the person who perfected them. The thinking of one person created friction among the various karate masters.

In Shoto-Kan Karate these questions or conflicts of thought are eliminated, for the knowledge is not of one individual and one mind. Through the efforts and leadership of Karate Master Funakoshi Gichin, there is the organization of movements and thoughts of many other karate masters of his time. Mr. Funakoshi spent many years of careful study of these masters' skills in developing Shoto-Kan Karate.

Shoto-Kan Karate involves twenty-nine kata,

each of which is more intricate than the last, each involves entirely different and separate movements, and each is more beautiful than the last. Some kata are very strong, very violent, and very powerful, whereas others are very graceful, very smooth, and very beautiful. Each serves its own purpose, each has its own separate merits. The study and perfection of one kata prepares the student for the next, right up the ladder to the rank of black belt and finally to master.

Karate was developed by the masters, through the centuries, by the application of techniques against definite attacks. These attacks were quite frequent and a part of their way of life. Those who survived these attacks did so by the proper application of the techniques they developed. These techniques were retained, for in actual proven use they were definitely effective. Other techniques were discarded, for injuries and sometimes death followed their application. These masters learned the hard, precise way the techniques of karate in order to survive.

The masters perfected karate. What fool is there today who can step forward and perfect perfection?

SHOTO-KAN KARATE

The power derived in the offensive and defensive movements in karate is accomplished by the dynamic tension (squeezing together as tightly as possible) of the muscles of the entire body at the moment of impact. This must be accomplished in the fastest possible time (split second during an attack). The movements of the body are controlled by the breathing. Any fast movement done by the body can only be performed by a quick exhalation of air from the lungs. In karate this exhalation is brought out very quickly by a loud scream or yell. This serves three purposes:

Dynamic Tension

1. It instantly brings one's ribs closer together, forming a tight protective shield for the internal organs against possible injury.

2. More important, it momentarily numbs the opponent's senses by the surprise of the loud scream or yell.

3. It concentrates all the power of the body to a striking point of not more than four or five inches in radius, whether it be a block, strike, or kick.

18

When properly applied, dynamic tension involves every muscle of the body. Here one can see the tension carried down to the feet, as the toes literally grip and become a part of the floor.

Warm-up Exercises

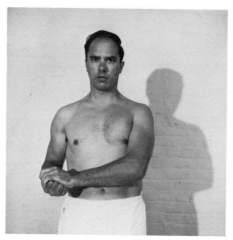 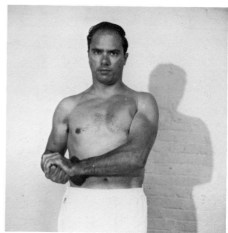

1. Stand perfectly upright. Place the right arm by the side of the body with the fist clenched, knuckles down, and bring the left arm across in front of the body and place the left hand over the right fist.

2. Tense all the muscles of the body as tightly as possible and simultaneously force the right fist up and the left palm down. Shift arm-and-hand positions and repeat the exercise on the opposite side. *Note:* The force of one hand is equalized by that of the other. All the muscles work against each other and, over a period of time, the power within the body increases. Simple as the exercise seems, if you stand in front of a mirror while performing it, you will see all the muscles of your body bulge and strain.

I

 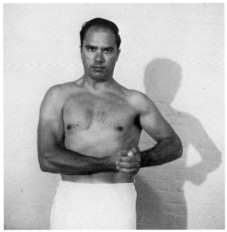

II

1. Stand perfectly upright. Place the right arm across the abdomen with the fist clenched, and place the left hand over the right fist.

2. Tense all the muscles of the body as tightly as possible and simultaneously force the right fist and left palm against each other. Shift arm-and-hand positions and repeat the exercise on the opposite side.

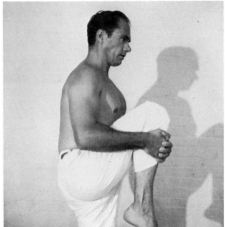

1. Stand perfectly upright. Bring the right knee up to the chest as high as possible and grasp it with both hands; the left hand overlapping the right. Tense all the muscles of the abdomen and point the toes of the right foot down. Pull the knee in hard against the chest and hold to the count of ten; then relax completely and repeat. Shift leg positions and repeat the exercise with the left.

2. Side view of the position in Fig. 1.

22

IV

1. Place two chairs shoulder-width apart. Place a hand on the edge of each chair and extend the feet back until the body is in a straight line.

2. Slowly dip between the chairs as far as possible and then push back up to the original position. *Note:* These push-ups should be done in sets of ten, and, because of the narrow space between the chairs, they will give depth to the chest.

1. Place two chairs two shoulder-widths apart.
Place a hand on the edge of each chair and extend
the feet back until the body is in a straight line.

2. Slowly dip between the chairs as far as possible
and then push back up to the original position.
Note: Since the chairs are farther apart, the strain
will be greater. (Care must be taken to limit these
push-ups to one's individual strength.) Although
Exercises IV and V appear similar, each affects
entirely different muscles. This exercise will de-
velop a very broad chest.

24

VI

1. Lie on the floor with the backs of both hands under the hips in order to elevate the base of the spine off the floor. Keep the legs perfectly straight and raise the feet about six inches off the floor.

2. Slowly raise the legs as high as possible and then slowly return them to their original position, with the feet about six inches above the floor. *Note:* These leg-raises should be done twenty times without stopping.

Stances

There are many positions, or stances, in karate: the forward-leaning stance, straddle-leg stance, back stance, etc. Each serves its own purpose, each is unique in its separate purpose. From any of these stances one is also capable of using kicking techniques. For example, in the forward-leaning stance the rear leg is brought up into a front-snap kick. As the kick is performed, the leg is momentarily fully extended giving one a driving force of about seven feet from rear to front. As the kicking leg completes its technique, it is brought down immediately into another forward-leaning stance, and one can then cover another seven feet by repeating the same technique with the opposite, rear leg.

FORWARD-LEANING STANCE

1. Bring the right leg forward twice the width of the shoulders, keeping both feet flat on the floor and the body perfectly upright and balanced. Bend the right leg at the knee and keep the left straight, with the toes turned out at a 45-degree angle away from the body.

2. Front view of the position in Fig. 1. *Note:* Both feet are in line with the edges of the shoulders.

STRADDLE-LEG STANCE

1. Spread the legs two shoulder-widths apart. Keep the feet flat on the floor and the knees bent outward. Turn the toes in slightly and grip the floor. *Note:* The body is perfectly balanced and upright, with the head in a line to the center of both feet.

2. Front view of the position in Fig. 1.

BACK STANCE

1. Bring the right leg forward twice the width of the shoulders and force the left backward, bending both legs at the knees and keeping both feet flat on the floor. *Note:* The body is perfectly balanced and upright, with the head in a line to the center of both feet.

2. Front view of the position in Fig. 1. *Note:* The toes of the right foot are pointing directly forward and the heel is lined up with that of the left. (The position facing the opponent is a side-front facing stance, which leaves as little of the body open to attack as possible.)

Blocking Techniques

Blocking movements in karate are not what they appear to be. An individual generally sees only the obvious: the blocking movement and nothing else. To every force moving in one direction there is an equal force moving in the opposite direction. An example of this can be seen in the simple firing of a firearm—the greater the grains of powder in the shell, the greater the force of the recoil. Such is the case in blocking techniques.

In a low block, for example, the right fist is brought up to the left side of the neck while the left arm is stretched completely out, with the fist directly in front of the groin. As the right fist is brought downward to perform a low block, the extended left arm is whipped back to the side of the body in a clenched fist. The damage done by the application of this simple technique is not by the blocking arm, but by the left arm being retracted to the side of the body. The result is a broken arm for the attacker.

(executed while in a forward-leaning stance)

1. Bring the right fist up to the left side of the neck and stretch the left arm out in front of the groin.

2. Bring the right fist down and simultaneously withdraw the left arm in to the side.

3. Upon completion of this technique, the right fist is directly over the right knee; the left arm is back firm against the side with the fist clenched. *Note:* The left arm must be parallel to the floor.

4. Side view of the position in Fig. 3.

1. In the low block the arm is stretched completely out and directly in front and is ready and capable of grabbing an opponent's wrist.

2. Retaining the hold on the wrist, as the arm is brought back by the side of the body, bring the right arm down in a low block.

3. This block is performed between the shoulder and elbow joints. The end result is a broken arm at the elbow joint.

The simple technique of grabbing the opponent's wrist can also be applied in an upper block. As the left arm performs the upper block, the hand is opened with the palm facing the opponent. This puts the open palm in a definite ready position for grabbing the opponent's wrist. As the blocking hand is brought back to the side of the body retaining the hold on the opponent's wrist, the right arm is whipped out in a punch to the body. Keep the grip on the opponent's wrist and he has no alternative but to fall over backward at the moment of the punch.

Again the damage is done by the retracting hand; in this case, the hold on the wrist by the left hand.

(executed while in a forward-leaning stance)

1. Bring the right arm in to the side and stretch the left out directly in front of the body, keeping both fists clenched.

2. Bring both arms up, forming an X, with the right on the outside.

3. Upon completion of this technique, the right forearm is at head level and the left has been retracted to the side. The palm of the right fist is facing forward and that of the left up. *Note:* Care must be taken not to cover the eyes with the right forearm. The left arm must be parallel to the floor.

4. Side view of the position in Fig. 3.

1. In the upper block, the palm is facing the opponent and is in a ready position to grip his wrist.

2. The grip on the wrist must be strong.

3. Maintain the grip on the opponent's wrist and bring the holding hand in to the side of the body, while simultaneously punching the opponent with the right fist.

4. The pull of one hand and the striking force of the other will put the opponent down on his back.

FOREARM BLOCK
(executed while in a forward-leaning stance)

1. Bring both fists out in front of the body at groin level.

2. Bring the right arm in up to chest level parallel to the floor, with the palm face down.

3. Simultaneously withdraw the left in to the side and drop the right elbow in to the side, forcing the right fist outward. *Note:* Upon completion of this technique, the right fist is at shoulder level, with the fingers of the fist facing the body. The left arm is parallel to the floor.

4. Side view of the position in Fig. 3.

1. Bring the palm of the right hand up to the left side of the neck and stretch the left arm out in front of the body, with the palm face down. *Note:* At this point the feet are close together.

2. Step into a right back stance, bringing the right arm out to the front and withdrawing the left. *Note:* All of these movements should be done simultaneously.

3. Upon completion of this technique, the palm of the right hand is parallel with the shoulders and the left is in front of the solar plexus. *Note:* The body must be perfectly balanced.

4. Side view of the position in Fig. 3.

Kicking Techniques

There are many techniques in karate which involve much leg work. In whatever technique a leg is used, the knee has complete control over the power of the kick, the manner in which it is delivered, and the height. If the knee is brought up only waist high, the kick will be only waist high. By driving the knee up against the chest as high as possible, one is capable of kicking at least to the height of the opponent's head. At the completion of the kick, the leg must be brought back to its original position prior to kicking before it can be returned to the floor.

By proper training under a master a kick connecting with an opponent in the lower part of his body can have devastating effects, especially with a shoe on.

FRONT-SNAP KICK
*(executed while in a
forward-leaning stance)*

1. The distance between the feet is approximately three to four feet.

2. There is a driving force of about seven feet from the rear to the opponent. The power of the kick is quite obvious.

45

FRONT-SNAP KICK *(attacking the groin)*

1. The height of the knee controls the height of the kick.

2. The point of contact here is the groin.

3. The toes of the kicking foot must be curled back in order to prevent injury to the toes. *Note:* The force of the blow is taken on the ball of the foot.

FRONT-SNAP KICK
(attacking the chin)

1. Again, the height of the knee controls the height of the kick.

2. Here, the knee was brought up much higher, with the point of contact being the opponent's chin.

SIDE-KICK *(attacking the lower region)*

1. In preparing for a side-kick aimed at the lower region, the knee is brought up very high in order to have as much downward momentum as possible.

2. The shock of the blow in a side-kick is absorbed on the edge of the foot.

3. The toes must be pulled back toward the body. This forces the ankle to tense up, which in turn absorbs the shock of the kick. *Note:* Perfect balance must be maintained or the force of the kick, upon contact, will throw you off-balance.

48

1. Again, the knee is brought up at least waist high. Balance is maintained on the supporting leg.

2. The point of impact is the opponent's throat. By keeping the proper distance from an opponent, he cannot come into contact with you since the legs are much longer than the arms.

BACK KICK

Contact is always made with the heel of the foot.
Note: The line of travel of the leg must be straight
backward or there will be a loss of force at the
moment of impact.

COMPLETION OF A TECHNIQUE

At the completion of a defensive movement, or
technique, one must instantly relax the muscles of
the entire body in order to be prepared for and to
perform the next technique whether it be an attack
or a defensive move.

The same can be said of a swimmer in a race—
if he were to remain continually tense from the
start, after a few moments he would sink to the
bottom. He must relax after each stroke in order
to move the body smoothly and continually in the
performance of the next stroke. And, so it is with
karate. If a person remained constantly tensed in
an attack, the muscles would tire, blood circula-
tion throughout the body would be obstructed by
the locked muscles, making freedom of movement
impossible, and he would sink in defeat.

51

KATA

Bassai No. 1

The position stated in this kata (Bassai No. 1) is with the wall on the left side of the body at a distance of four feet. This has been done merely for the demonstration of the kata in this book and is not, of course, standard procedure in the general performance of the kata.

1. Stand in a formal stance with the feet about four inches apart; toes pointed slightly outward.

2. Raise the right knee about chest high. Place the right fist beside the left ear and stretch the left arm out directly in front of the body.

3. Step straight forward and place the right foot down and bring the left foot up behind the right heel, keeping the heel off the floor. Simultaneously execute a back-fist strike with the right hand. *Note:* The body must be perfectly balanced in a line from the head to the right foot. The left leg must be tight up against the calf of the right leg, and only the toes of the left foot are in contact with the floor. The palm of the left hand is facing directly forward.

Front view of the position in Fig. 3.

56

1. (2) The defense is started as the opponent begins the attack.

2. (3) The right hand executes a back-fist strike to the nose while the left hand brushes aside the opponent's right arm. *Note:* Both hands must make contact simultaneously.

4. Pivot to the left 180 degrees on the ball of the right foot and step into a left-leaning stance, placing the left fist by the right ear and stretching the right arm out directly in front of the body.

5. Bring the left arm forward with the fist clenched, executing a left outside-forearm block. *Note:* The right arm is brought back to the side with the fist clenched.

6. Bring the right arm forward and cross it over the left. *Note:* The right is on the outside.

7. Bring the left arm back to the side and simultaneously execute a right outside-forearm block.

58

Application of Left and Right Outside-Forearm Blocks *(see Figs. 4, 5, 6, and 7 opposite page)*

1. (4) As the opponent advances, prepare to meet his left-handed attack.

2. (5) Block the opponent's left punch with a left outside-forearm block. *Note:* The timing of the block must coincide with the opponent's attack.

3. (6) Cross the arms in preparation for a right outside-forearm block.

4. (7) As the opponent attacks with the opposite arm, execute a right outside-forearm block.

8. Pivot to the right 180 degrees on the balls of both feet into a right-leaning stance and execute a left outside-forearm block.

9. Upon completion of the movement, the left fist is in line with the left shoulder, and the body must be perfectly centered and balanced and the shoulders squared.

10. Bring the right arm forward and cross it over the left. *Note:* The right arm is on the outside.

11. Execute a right inside-forearm block. *Note:* The left arm is simultaneously brought back to the side.

60

Application of a Left Outside-Forearm Block and a Right Inside-Forearm Block
(see Figs. 8, 9, and 11 opposite page)

1. (8) As the opponent attacks from the rear, pivot to the right on the balls of both feet to meet the attack.

2. (9) Execute a left outside-forearm block as the opponent punches with his right.

3. (11) As the opponent attacks again, with his left, execute a right inside-forearm block.

4. Upon completion of any of these blocks, the blocking hand can be used to grab the opponent's clothing and pull him forward into a punch delivered by the other hand.

61

12. Bring the right foot back parallel with the left. *Note:* The body must be perfectly balanced, with the knees slightly bent.

13. Step to the right 90 degrees into a right-leaning stance and begin a low-scooping block from left to right with the right arm.

14. Continue scooping to the right.

15. Continue the scooping block to the right and upward, bringing the fist to shoulder level. *Note:* At this point the left hand must be brought forward.

Application of a Right Low-Scooping Block
(see Figs. 12 and 14 opposite page)

1. (12) As the opponent attacks with a right front-snap kick, step into a right-leaning stance (Fig. 13) directly toward the attack.

2. (14) Scoop the opponent's right foot to the right and upward (Fig. 15), throwing him off-balance.

16. Press the left-hand palm down against the right biceps. *Note:* The body is still in the right-leaning stance.

17. Bring the right arm directly across the front of the chest, executing a right inside-forearm block, and draw the left arm back to the side with clenched fist.

Application of a Right-Scooping Block and
a Body Drop *(see Fig. 16 opposite page)*

1. (16) Press the palm of the left hand against the
opponent's leg, locking it against the right arm.
Note: The opponent's balance is in your control.

2. Shift the left hand to the opponent's shoulder
and grab his clothing.

3. Simultaneously pull with the left hand and
shove with the right forearm.

4. The force of your pulling and shoving will drop
the opponent to the floor on his back.

18. Cross the left arm over the right. *Note:* The left arm must be on the outside.

19. Execute a left inside-forearm block and draw the right arm back to the side. *Note:* The position is still the right-leaning stance, and the shoulder must be squared directly to the front of the block.

pplication of a Left Inside-Forearm Block
e Figs. 18 and 19 opposite page)

(18) As the forearms cross, the fists must be at
oulder level. The blocking arm, in this case the
't, must be on the outside.

(19) The timing of the block must coincide
th the opponent's attack.

20. Bring the right foot back to the left 90 degrees parallel with the left and bring both fists together by the right side at waist level.

21. Slowly swing the left arm out, with open palm, in a circular motion directly to the front of the body.

22. Execute a left palm-heel block and step into a straddle-leg stance. *Note:* The body must be perfectly balanced, with the head in a line to the center of both feet. The left palm must be parallel to an imaginary wall directly to the front and the right fist must be tightly clenched by the side.

Application of a Left Palm-Heel Block
(see Figs. 20, 21, and 22 opposite page)

1. (20) Prepare for an anticipated attack.

2. (21) As the opponent steps closer in his attack, swing the left arm out in a circular motion.

3. (22) As the opponent punches out with his right, execute a left palm-heel block. *Note:* The shock of the attack is sustained strictly by the straddle-leg stance; the toes grip the floor as tightly as possible.

23. Punch out with the right fist directly forward at nose level and simultaneously withdraw the left arm to the side.

24. Pivot to the left 90 degrees on the balls of both feet into a left-leaning stance and simultaneously execute a right-forearm block directly to the right.

Note: The feet must not move from their original position when pivoting; the forearm block is executed directly to the right where the punch has just been delivered.

25. Pivot to the right on the balls of both feet and step into a straddle-leg stance and simultaneously punch out directly forward with the left fist.

Application of a Right Straight Punch, Right Inside-Forearm Block, and Left Straight Punch *(see Figs. 23, 24, and 25 opposite page)*

1. (23) Grab the opponent's right forearm with your left hand, pulling him toward you and simultaneously punching out with the right fist directly to his nose.

2. (24) As the opponent lashes out with his opposite arm, pivot to the left and execute a right inside-forearm block.

3. (25) Grab the opponent's left forearm with your right hand and simultaneously punch out with the left fist directly to the nose.

26. Pivot to the right 90 degrees on the balls of both feet into a right-leaning stance and execute a left inside-forearm block. *Note:* The feet must not move from their original position when pivoting; the forearm block is executed directly to the left where the punch has just been delivered.

27. Bring the feet together by moving the left in and drawing the right back in front of the left, with the heel off the floor. Stretch the left arm directly out to the front of the body and place the palm of the right hand by the left side of the neck. *Note:* Balance must be maintained at all times.

28. Step forward with the right leg in preparation to stepping into a right-back stance and bring the right arm forward, palm in, in preparation to executing a knife-hand block, and withdraw the left back to the side.

Application of a Left Inside-Forearm Block
(see Figs. 26 and 27 opposite page)

1. (26) Again, as the opponent punches out with the right fist, execute a left inside-forearm block.

2. (27) As the opponent renews his attack, bring the feet together in preparation to stepping into a right-back stance.

29. Step into a right-back stance and execute a right knife-hand block. *Note:* The right hand is at shoulder level; the toes of the right foot are pointing directly to the front of the body, and the left hand is open and parallel to the floor with the palm face up.

30. Bring the left foot forward slightly in front of the right, with the heel off the floor. Stretch the right arm directly out to the front of the body and place the palm of the left hand alongside the right side of the neck.

31. Step forward with the left leg in preparation to stepping into a left-back stance and bring the left arm forward, palm in, in preparation to executing a knife-hand block, and withdraw the right back to the side.

32. Step into a left-back stance and execute a left knife-hand block. *Note:* The left hand is at shoulder level; the toes of the left foot are pointing directly to the front of the body, and the right hand is open and parallel to the floor with the palm face up.

Application of Right and Left Knife-Hand Blocks
and Counterattacks
(see Figs. 29 and 32 opposite page)

1. (29) As the opponent punches out with his left,
step into a right-back stance and execute a right
knife-hand block.

2. Grab the opponent's left forearm with your
right and pivot into a right-leaning stance directly
toward him and simultaneously send a spear-hand
thrust to his throat just below the Adam's apple.

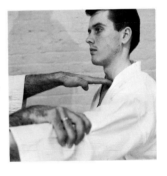

Close-up of spear-hand thrust to the throat.

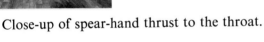

3. (32) As the opponent punches out with his
other hand, step into a left-back stance and execute a left knife-hand block.

4. Grab the opponent's right forearm with your
left and deliver a left front-snap kick to his face.
Note: Balance must be maintained on the right
leg.

33. Bring the right foot forward slightly in front of the left, with the heel off the floor. Stretch the left arm directly out to the front of the body and place the palm of the right hand alongside the left side of the neck. *Note:* These movements are preparatory to stepping into a right-back stance and executing a right knife-hand block.

34. Step into a right-back stance and execute a right knife-hand block. *Note:* There are three back stances with the knife-hand block which move continuously forward. A fourth (Figs. 35 and 36) moves backward.

35. Bring the right foot back to the left. Stretch the right arm directly out to the front of the body and place the palm of the left hand alongside the right side of the neck. *Note:* Both feet must be parallel with each other.

36. Keep the left foot firmly planted. Step backward with the right leg in preparation to stepping into a left-back stance and bring the left arm forward, palm in, in preparation to executing a knife-hand block, and withdraw the right back to the side.

Application of a Right Knife-Hand Block and Its Completion *(see Fig. 34 opposite page)*

1. (34) As the opponent punches out with his right, execute a right knife-hand block.

2. Grab the opponent's right wrist with your right hand and pivot into a right-leaning stance, pulling with your right and pushing against the opponent's right shoulder with your left hand. *Note:* The opponent has two choices—either go down or receive a broken elbow.

37. Step back into a left-back stance and execute a left knife-hand block while stepping directly to the rear.

38. Pivot directly forward into a left-leaning stance to the front of the knife-hand block just completed. Keep the left arm at the same height, facing directly forward, in front of the body and bring the right arm forward directly from the solar plexus.

39. Execute a circular movement with the right hand from right to left. *Note*. The left hand begins its movement toward the right upper forearm; the left arm overlaps the right.

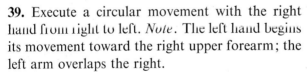

40. At the completion of this movement, the palm of the right hand is facing directly out to the front at shoulder level and the palm of the left hand is pressed tightly against the right upper forearm. *Note:* The body must be perfectly balanced and centered in the execution of this technique.

78

Application of an Interlocking Block
(see Figs. 37, 38, 39, and 40 opposite page)

1. (37) As the opponent punches out with his right, execute a left knife-hand block.

2. (38) Pivot into a left-leaning stance and bring the left hand to the outside of the opponent's right forearm.

3. (39) Bring the right hand up under the opponent's right forearm.

4. (40) Interlock both hands to the outside of the opponent's forearm. *Note:* The left arm is over the right; the left hand presses the opponent's right wrist to your upper forearm and the right clutches his forearm.

79

41. Keep the arms locked in position and bring the right knee forward and up to waist level.

42. Pivot to the left on the ball of the left foot so that the toes point almost to the rear, and side-thrust with the right. Simultaneously bring both hands up tight against the right side of the body about waist high. *Note:* The thrust of the right leg is not upward; it is directed in a definite downward angle and is aimed at the opponent's right hip joint.

43. Maintain balance on the left leg and bring the right back so that the knee is again at waist level. Stretch the right arm to the left and place the palm of the left hand by the right side of the neck.

Side view of the position in Fig. 43.

Application of Interlocking Block and Counter-attack *(see Figs. 41 and 42 opposite page)*

1. (41) Maintain your grip on the opponent's right forearm and bring the right knee up.

2. (42) Pull on the opponent's right arm with boths hands and simultaneously drive the right foot down into his right hip joint.

Front view of the technique in Fig. 2.

44. Drop the right leg backward, stepping into a left-back stance, and bring the left arm forward at shoulder level, executing a left knife-hand block.

45. Bring the right leg forward and step directly into a right-back stance and execute a right knife-hand block.

Application of a Left Knife-Hand Block, Right Palm-Heel Strike, Right Knife-Hand Block, and Left Spear-Hand Thrust
(see Figs. 44 and 45 opposite page)

1. (44) As the opponent advances punching out with his right, step backward into a left-back stance and execute a left knife-hand block.

2. Grip the opponent's right forearm with your left hand and pivot directly forward into a left-leaning stance, simultaneously striking his chin with the heel of your right hand.

3. (45) As the opponent punches out again, with his left, step forward into a right-back stance and execute a right knife-hand block.

4. Grip the opponent's left forearm (or sleeve) with your right hand and pivot directly forward into a right-leaning stance, simultaneously sending a left spear-hand thrust to his solar plexus.

83

46. Bring the right foot back parallel with the left, and clench the fists of both hands in front of the groin.

47. Raise both fists upward in unison.

48. Continue raising the fists until they are well above the head. *Note:* The elbows must be bent and the fists must be parallel with each other and tightly clenched.

Front view of the position in Fig. 48.

Application of a Double-Fist Block
(see Figs. 46, 47, and 48 opposite page)

1. (46) As the opponent advances reaching for your neck with both hands, step back with the right leg, bringing both fists forward and up.

2. (47–48) As the opponent closes in, bring your arms up inside his. *Note:* The bend in your elbows will force the opponent's arms apart, thus breaking the force of his attack.

Top view of the technique in Fig. 2.

49. Break the fists apart to the left and right. *Note:* The fists must be parallel with each other and the forearms must be perpendicular to the floor; thus the arms form a square.

Front view of the position in Fig. 49.

Application of Breaking the Opponent's Arms
Apart with the Double-Fist Block
(see Fig. 49 opposite page)

Break the arms apart, forcing the opponent's
arms out to each side.

50. Raise the right knee chest high and simultaneously bring both fists down forward, maintaining balance on the left leg.

Front view of the position in Fig. 50.

51. Drop forward into a right-leaning stance, simultaneously opening the left fist and striking the palm with the right fist. *Note:* The strike is executed level with the solar plexus.

Front view of the position in Fig. 51.

88

Application of a Double Knife-Hand Strike
(see Figs. 50 and 51 opposite page)

1. (50) Open the palms of both hands while stepping forward into a right-leaning stance.

2. (51) Strike the opponent on both sides of the rib cage with the edges of both hands simultaneously.

52. Hold the right fist against the palm of the left hand and bring the left foot forward even with the right.

53. Step directly forward into a right-leaning stance and punch out with the right fist.

54. Look to the left directly to the rear and raise the right arm well above the head and drop the left to the rear, with the palm face down.

55. Pivot to the left on the balls of both feet into a left-leaning stance and raise the left arm. *Note:* The palms of both hands are facing in the direction of the stance.

Application of a Right Fore-Fist Strike
(see Figs. 52, 53, 54, and 55 opposite page)

1. (52) Grab the opponent's clothing with the left hand.

2. (53) Retain the hold and step forward into a right-leaning stance and deliver a right fore-fist strike to the opponent's heart.

3. (54) Look back over the left shoulder and prepare for an attack (from another opponent) from the rear.

4. (55) Step into a left-leaning stance so that you face the opponent head on. *Note:* The palms of both hands face the opponent.

91

56. Strike directly forward at waist level with the right hand, palm up, simultaneously bringing the left hand, palm out, up to the right shoulder. *Note:* The palm of the right hand is face up and forward. The palm of the left is face out alongside the right shoulder. The body must be perfectly balanced, with the head in a line to the center of both feet.

57. Return to a left-back stance and bring the right arm back with clenched fist and simultaneously whip the left arm down into a low block, also with the fist clenched.

58. Raise the right arm up to the back. *Note:* The right upper arm is perpendicular to the floor and the fist is held at head level.

Application of a Left Palm-Heel Block, Right Knife-Hand Strike, Counterattack, and a Body Drop *(see Fig. 56 opposite page)*

1. (56) Brush aside the opponent's right-handed attack with the palm of your left hand and simultaneously deliver a right knife-hand strike to his groin.

2. Grab the opponent's clothing at the shoulder with your left hand and in the groin area (or by the belt as illustrated) with your right.

3. Bring your left foot up to the rear of the opponent's forward foot, in this case his right.

4. Shove with your left hand and pull with your right, simultaneously whipping your left foot back to the right, dropping the opponent to the floor on his back.

59. Bring the left foot back parallel with the right.

60. Pivot to the left 90 degrees on the ball of the left foot and bring the right knee up to chest level. *Note:* The left arm remains extended and the right fist is brought up to the left side of the neck. Both arms must be stretched to the utmost; balance is maintained on the left leg.

61. Pivot to the left another 90 degrees and drop into a straddle-leg stance and execute a right low block directly to the right.

Side view of the position in Fig. 61.

Application of a Right Low Block
(see Figs. 59, 60, and 61 opposite page)

1. (59) Step back with the left foot in preparation for an anticipated right front-snap kick attack.

2. (60) Pivot to the left, raising the right knee before the opponent's kick is half completed.

3. (61) Execute a low block from a straddle-leg stance to the outside of the opponent's right leg.

62. Stretch the right arm to the left across the chest, palm down, and place the palm of the left hand by the right side of the neck.

63. Slowly swing the left arm out in a circular arc at shoulder level, executing a back-hand block and simultaneously bring the right arm back to the side.

64. Extend the left arm to the left at shoulder level. *Note:* The entire technique is executed very slowly.

Side view of the position in Fig. 64.

Application of a Left Back-Hand Block
(see Figs. 62 and 64 opposite page)

1. (62) As the opponent advances, prepare to execute a left back-hand block against his right-handed attack.

2. (64) Block his right arm with a left back-hand block.

65. Pivot to the left 90 degrees on the left foot, bringing the right forward and up, kicking the palm of the left hand with the right foot. *Note:* The right foot travels in a 180-degree arc. The palm of the left hand must be stationary. From the heel to the back of the knee joint, the right leg must be parallel to the floor. The right arm is locked to the side.

Front view of the position in Fig. 65.

66. Upon completion of the kick, instantly drop the right leg down and step into a straddle-leg stance, simultaneously striking the right elbow with the palm of the left hand. *Note:* The fist of the inside arm, the right, is clenched and both arms are parallel to the floor.

Application of a Counterattack with a Right Crescent-Kick and a Right Elbow-Strike *(see Figs. 65 and 66 opposite page)*

1. (65) Grab the opponent's right arm with your left hand and deliver a right crescent-kick to his heart. *Note:* The bottom of the foot is the striking point.

2. Maintain your hold on the opponent's arm and withdraw the right leg before dropping it to the floor.

3. (66) Still holding on to the opponent's arm, step down into a straddle-leg stance and deliver a right elbow-strike to his chest.

67. Execute a right low block and clench the fist of the left hand. *Note:* The left arm remains parallel to the floor about one foot out in front of the chest.

68. Execute a left low block, simultaneously bringing the right arm back to in front of the chest, also about one foot away.

69. Execute another right low block.

70. Pivot to the right on the balls of both feet and bring both fists in to the left side. *Note:* The right fist must be in front of the left.

100

Application of Low Blocks Against Kicks
(see Figs. 67, 68, and 69 opposite page)

1. (67) Right low block against left kick.

2. (68) Left low block against right kick.

3. (69) Right low block against left kick.

71. Strike directly forward with both fists in unison, executing a double-fist punch. *Note:* The right fist is aimed at the midsection; the left at the forehead.

72. At the completion of the punch, the body faces directly forward in line with the punch and both fists are perpendicular with each other.

Front view of the position in Fig. 72.

73. Bring the right foot back parallel with the left and bring both fists down to the right side, with the left fist in front of the right.

102

Application of a Double-Fist Punch
(see Figs. 71 and 72 opposite page)

1. (71) As the attack is begun, both fists leave the right side in unison.

2. (72) The left arm executes a high block and a fore-fist strike to the opponent's head as the right fist strikes his midsection.

103

74. Maintain balance on the right leg and bring the left knee up to chest level.

75. Execute a left front-snap kick. *Note:* The body must not lean forward while executing the kick and must be centered with the left leg in order to maintain proper balance.

76. Upon completion of the kick, drop directly forward into a left-leaning stance and execute a double-fist punch.

77. Upon completion of the double-fist punch, both fists are perpendicular with each other and the body faces directly forward in line with the punch. *Note:* The body must be perfectly balanced, with the head in a line to the center of both feet.

Application of a Left Front-Snap Kick, Double-Fist Punch, Counterattack, and a Body Drop *(see Figs. 75 and 76 opposite page)*

1. (75) As the opponent advances, deliver a left front-snap kick to his face.

2. (76) Before he can recover, drop forward into a left-leaning stance and deliver a double-fist punch to his forehead and midsection.

3. Grip the opponent's clothing at the shoulder with your right hand and his trousers (or belt) with your left.

4. Bring your right foot up to the rear of the opponent's forward foot, in this case his left.

5. Shove with your right hand and pull with your left, simultaneously whipping your right foot back to the rear, dropping the opponent to the floor on his back.

105

78. Bring the left foot back parallel with the right and bring both fists down to the left side, with the right in front of the left.

79. Execute a right front-snap kick.

80. Upon completion of the kick, drop forward into a right-leaning stance and execute a double-fist punch.

Front view of the position in Fig. 80.

Application of a Right Front-Snap Kick and a Double-Fist Punch
(see Figs. 79 and 80 opposite page)

1. (79) As the opponent advances, deliver a right front-snap kick to his face.

2. (80) Before he can recover, drop forward into a right-leaning stance and deliver a double-fist punch to his forehead and midsection.

81. Pivot to the left on the right foot and swing the left leg back so that the body is facing in the opposite direction. *Note:* The position at this point is a right-leaning stance, with both arms stretched to the right and parallel to the floor.

82. Continue pivoting to the left, bringing the left arm up to the side and executing a low-scooping block with the right arm.

83. Upon completion of the block, the right forearm is parallel to the floor.

Application of a Right Inside-Scooping Block and Body Drop *(see Figs. 82 and 83 opposite page)*

1. (82) As the opponent attacks with a left front-snap kick, hook his leg in a low-scooping block with your right arm.

2. (83) Apply force to the right and downward, and the opponent will drop to the floor on his back.

84. Pivot to the right on the balls of both feet into a right-leaning stance and execute a left inside-scooping block.

85. Upon completion of the block, the left forearm is parallel to the floor.

Application of a Left Inside-Scooping Block and Body Drop *(see Figs. 84 and 85 opposite page)*

1. (84) As the opponent attacks with a right front-snap kick, hook his leg in a low-scooping block with your left arm.

2. Apply force to the left and downward.

3. (85) The opponent will drop to the floor on his back.

Close-up of the technique in Fig. 3.

86. Bring the left foot forward and cross it in front of the right, which remains firmly planted. Place the palm of the right hand by the left side of the neck and stretch the left arm directly out to the front with the palm face down.

87. Step forward with the right leg into a right-back stance and execute a right knife-hand block, withdrawing the left hand, palm up, to in front of the solar plexus.

88. Swing the right leg to the right, pivoting on the left foot. *Note:* The arms do not change positions, only the body.

Application of a Right Knife-Hand Block and a Left Knife-Hand Strike
(see Figs. 86 and 87 opposite page)

1. (86) As the opponent advances, prepare to block a right-handed attack.

2. (87) Step forward into a right-back stance and execute a right knife-hand block to the outside of the opponent's attacking arm.

3. Grip the opponent's right wrist with your right hand and pivot into a right-leaning stance. Simultaneously raise the left hand well above the head in a knife-hand striking position.

4. Keeping the grip on the opponent's wrist, strike his arm between the shoulder and elbow joints with the edge of your left hand. *Note:* The opponent's arm will break at the elbow joint, if you are not careful.

89. Bring the right foot back and cross it in front of the left, which remains firmly planted.

90. Step forward with the left leg into a left-back stance and execute a left knife-hand block, withdrawing the right hand, palm up, to in front of the solar plexus. *Note:* In this movement the preparation of the arms for the block is omitted. The forward momentum of the stance is augmented by the swinging of the arms, in unison, in the execution of the block.

91. Bring the left foot back up to the right, returning to a formal stance.

114

Application of an Augmented Right Knife-Hand
Strike *(see Fig. 89 opposite page)*

1. (89) As the opponent moves in, double-step in his direction.

2. Left foot advanced.

3. The blocking of the left hand and the striking of the right are done in one, smooth continuous movement. *Note:* The entire force of the body weight is driven into the right knife-hand strike.

115

An example in the understanding of the movements of karate would be two people beginning the study of a musical instrument at the same time. Given the same amount of study, one would merely qualify as a musician, whereas the other would have the touch of the master.

The student who has achieved the master's touch is the one who had the will to go beyond the point of the average and delve into the deeper and more satisfying technique of the instrument he has chosen.

The instrument, in this case, is karate.

KATA

Tekki No. 1

The kata (Tekki No. 1) on the following pages is very unique. It is designed for defense against attack with one's back to the wall. The shifting of positions are parallel to the wall thus leaving one to concentrate his defense to the left, right, and directly forward. The wall covering his back is his greatest defense.

1. Stand in a formal stance with the feet about four inches apart; toes pointed slightly outward. *Note:* The body is relaxed.

2. Step to the right with the left foot, crossing it in front of the right. Keep the feet close together, with the knees slightly bent. *Note:* The hands are open with the palms facing inward; fingertips touching.

3. Balance the body on the left leg and bring the right knee up as high as possible. *Note:* The body must not be bent or distorted, and balance is maintained on the left leg. The right knee must be to the outside of the right elbow.

4. Keeping the left leg slightly bent and the hands locked in position, front-snap kick with the right leg. *Note:* The kick is directed at a 45-degree angle to the left away from the line of travel.

Application of a Right Front-Snap Kick
(see Figs. 2, 3, and 4 opposite page)

1. (2) As the opponent begins the attack, double-step in his direction.

2. (3) Raise the right knee as high as possible in preparation for the kick.

3. (4) Deliver a right front-snap kick to the opponent's chin. *Note:* Contact is made with the ball of the foot.

123

5. At the completion of the right front-snap kick, drop the right leg directly to the right, stepping into a straddle-leg stance. At the instant the right foot touches the floor, swing the right arm out in an arc at shoulder level, executing a back-hand block.

6. As the right arm blocks, bring the left back to the side with clenched fist. *Note:* The toes must be tucked inward and pointed directly forward. The knees must be bent with the tension directed to the outside. The body must be balanced, with the head in a line to the center of both feet.

7. Start bringing the left arm forward to the right.

8. Pivot the body to the right from the waist up and drive your left elbow into the palm of the right hand. *Note:* Both arms must be parallel to the floor when contact is made. The strike is directly to the right. The strike derives its force from the twisting of the hips only. The feet and knees remain stationary.

124

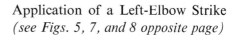
Application of a Left-Elbow Strike
(see Figs. 5, 7, and 8 opposite page)

1. (5) As the opponent advances, swing the right arm out.

2. (7) Block the opponent's left-handed attack with a right back-hand block.

3. (8) Grab the opponent's right arm with your right hand and pull him forward into a left elbow-strike.

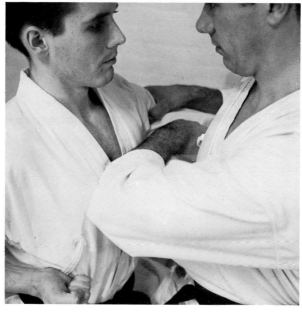

Close-up of the technique in Fig. 3.

9. Look to the left and bring both hands with clenched fists down to the right side, the right in front of the left.

10. Whip the left arm down to the left in a low block.

11. Upon completion of the block, the left arm is directly to the left and the right is stationary by the side.

12. Swing the right fist in a circular strike directly in front of the solar plexus and withdraw the left arm to the side.

Application of a Left Low Block
(see Figs. 10 and 11 opposite page)

1. (10) As the opponent attacks with a right front-snap kick, bring the left arm down hard.

2. (11) Execute a left low block, knocking aside the opponent's attacking leg. *Note:* The blocking hand must be tightly clenched in order to prevent injury to the fingers when contact is made.

13. Bring the right arm across the chest about one foot away from the body. Withdraw the left arm back to the side. *Note:* The right forearm is parallel to the floor. The body is perfectly balanced, with the head in a line to the center of both feet.

14. Look to the left and step to the left with the right foot, crossing it in front of the left. Keep the feet close together, with the knees slightly bent.

15. Balance the body on the right leg and bring the left knee up as high as possible.

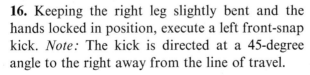

16. Keeping the right leg slightly bent and the hands locked in position, execute a left front-snap kick. *Note:* The kick is directed at a 45-degree angle to the right away from the line of travel.

128

Application of a Right Fore-Fist Strike and a Left Front-Snap Kick

(see Figs. 15 and 16 opposite page)

1. As the opponent drops forward upon completion of the kick, deliver a right fore-fist strike to his chest.

2. (15) Raise the left knee in preparation for a front-snap kick.

3. (16) Deliver a left front-snap kick to the opponent's face.

17. At the completion of the kick, drop the left foot down directly to the left, with the toes tucked inward and the knees slightly bent. At the instant the left foot touches the floor, whip the right arm up into an inside-forearm block. *Note:* The fist of the right hand must be lined up with the right shoulder.

18. Cross the left arm with the right.

19. Swing the right arm down in a low block and the left arm up in an upper block. *Note:* Both arms must start and stop at the same time.

20. Bring the left hand down in a back-fist strike directly to the front at shoulder level and simultaneously bring the right arm up, with the back of the fist coming into contact with the left elbow. *Note:* The right arm is parallel to the floor and about one foot away from the body.

Application of a Right Inside-Forearm Block,
Left Upper Block, Right Solar-Plexus Punch, and
a Left Back-Fist Strike
(see Figs. 17 and 19 opposite page)

1. (17) As the opponent punches out with his left, execute a right inside-forearm block.

2. (19) As the opponent lashes out again, with his right hand, execute a left upper block and simultaneously whip your right fist into his solar plexus from the forearm-block position. *Note:* The block and punch must be executed in unison.

3. As the opponent punches out again with his left, brush his arm aside at the elbow with your right arm and whip the left fist down into a back-fist strike to his nose.

131

21. Snap the bottom of the left foot up directly in front of the body. *Note:* The foot must come up level with the pelvis area and must be returned to its original position fast enough to catch your balance, or you will fall to the left.

22. At the same instant the left foot returns to the floor, pivot the body to the left from the waist up and execute a left inside-forearm block, the force of which is directly to the left.

23. Snap the bottom of the right foot up directly in front of the body. *Note:* The upper body and arms do not change positions.

Application of a Left Inside-Snapping Block, Left
Inside-Forearm Block, and Right Fore-Fist Strike
(see Figs. 21 and 22 opposite page)

1. (21) As the opponent starts a right kick to your groin, block the attack with a left inside-snapping block.

2. The attack is now to the left.

3. (22) Block the opponent's right-handed attack with a left inside-forearm block and simultaneously deliver a right fore-fist strike to his chest.

133

24. Immediately return the right foot to its original position and pivot the body to the right from the waist up and execute a right inside-forearm block, all in one continuous movement.

25. At this point the right arm must be at shoulder level. *Note:* The blocking force is directly to the right.

26. Look to the left and bring both fists in to the right side, the left in front of the right.

27. Strike to the left at shoulder level with both fists simultaneously. *Note:* Do not move the body in the direction of the strike.

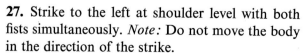

134

Application of a Right Inside-Forearm Block and Left Fore-Fist Strike
(see Figs. 24 and 25 opposite page)

1. (24) Start pivoting to meet the opponent's attack, which is now to the right.

2. (25) Block the opponent's left-handed attack with a right inside-forearm block and simultaneously deliver a left fore-fist strike to his chest.

28. At this point the right arm is directly in front of the chest, and both arms are parallel to the floor.

29. Upon completion of the strike, both arms are at shoulder level. *Note:* Both fists must start and stop at the same time.

30. Leave the right arm outstretched and open the palm, face down, and bring the left palm back alongside the right ear.

31. Slowly swing the left arm out in a circular arc at shoulder level, executing a back-hand block and simultaneously start bringing the right arm back to the side.

Application of a Left Low Block and Right Fore-Fist Strike and Left Back-Hand Block
(see Figs. 29, 30, and 31 opposite page)

1. As the opponent begins a right front-snap kick, prepare to meet the attack.

2. Block the kick with the left arm and deliver a right fore-fist strike (29) to the opponent's chest over the heart.

3. (30) Bring the left hand up alongside the right ear in preparation for a new attack.

4. (31) Block the opponent's right-handed attack with a left back-hand block.

32. At this point the left hand is extended at shoulder level and the right arm is withdrawn with clenched fist back to the side, hard enough to feel the strain in the shoulder muscles. *Note:* The body must be perfectly balanced.

33. Keep the lower part of the body stationary and pivot the upper part to the left from the waist up, bringing the right elbow out and the left forearm in.

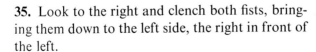

34. Drive the right elbow into the palm of the left hand. *Note:* Both arms must be parallel to the floor. The strike derives its force from the pivoting only and is directly to the left.

35. Look to the right and clench both fists, bringing them down to the left side, the right in front of the left.

Application of a Left Back-Hand Block and a
Right Elbow-Strike
(see Figs. 32, 34, and 35 opposite page)

1. (32) The blocking is done with the back of the left hand.

2. (34) Grab the opponent's clothing at the shoulder with your blocking hand and pull him forward into a right elbow-strike.

3. (35) Prepare for an attack from the opposite direction.

139

36. Whip the right arm down directly to the right into a low block.

37. At this point the right arm must be directly to the right while the left remains stationary by the side.

38. Swing the left fist out in a circular strike directly in front of the solar plexus and withdraw the right arm in to the side.

39. At this point the left arm must be parallel to the floor and about one foot away from the body, with the fist facing down; the right arm, with clenched fist, is back firmly against the side, knuckles down. *Note:* The body must be balanced, with the head in a line to the center of both feet.

140

Application of a Right Low Block and a Left Fore-Fist Strike *(see Fig. 37 opposite page)*

1. (37) Block the opponent's left front-snap kick to the right of the defense position.

2. As the opponent drops forward, block his left arm with your right and deliver a left fore-fist strike to his face.

40. Look to the right and cross the left foot over in front of the right, keeping the feet close together, with the knees slightly bent.

41. Keeping the left leg slightly bent and the hands locked in position, raise the right knee as high as possible.

42. Execute a right front-snap kick at face level. *Note:* The kick is directed at a 45-degree angle to the left away from the line of travel, which is to the right.

43. Upon completion of the kick, drop the right foot down directly to the right, with the toes turned inward and the knee slightly bent. At the instant the right foot touches the floor, whip the left arm up into an inside-forearm block. *Note:* The fist of the left hand must be lined up with the left shoulder.

Application of a Right Front-Snap Kick and a
Left Inside-Forearm Block
(see Figs. 41, 42, and 43 opposite page)

1. (41) As the opponent advances, raise the right
knee as high as possible.

2. (42) As the opponent attacks with his right
fist, front-snap kick his wrist with the right foot.

3. (43) As the opponent attacks with his right
again, knock aside his arm with a left inside-
forearm block.

44. Cross the left arm in front of the body with the right. *Note:* The right arm is on the outside.

45. Swing the left arm down into a low block and simultaneously execute an upper block with the right. *Note:* Both arms must start and stop at the same time.

46. Bring the right fist down in a back-fist strike directly to the front at shoulder level and simultaneously bring the left arm up across the chest until the fist makes contact with the right elbow. *Note:* The left arm is parallel to the floor about one foot away from the body.

47. Holding the arms in this position, snap the bottom of the right foot up directly in front of the body, level with the pelvis area.

Application of a Right Upper Block and Left
Fore-Fist Strike; Left Low Block and Right Back-
Fist Strike *(see Figs. 45 and 46 opposite page)*

1. (45) As the opponent punches out with his left,
execute a right upper block and deliver a left
fore-fist strike to his solar plexus.

2. (46) As the opponent punches out again, with
his right, block his arm with a left low block and
deliver a right back-fist strike to his nose.

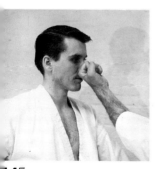

Close-up of back-fist strike to the nose in Fig. 2.

48. Immediately return the right foot to its original position and simultaneously pivot the upper body to the right from the waist up and execute a right inside-forearm block. *Note:* The forearm must execute the block the instant the right foot touches the floor. The right arm must be at shoulder level; the blocking force is directed to the right.

49. Holding this position, snap the bottom of the left foot up directly in front of the body, level with the pelvis area.

50. Immediately return the left foot to its original position and simultaneously pivot the upper body to the left from the waist up and execute a left inside-forearm block. *Note:* The forearm must execute the block the instant the left foot touches the floor. The left arm must be at shoulder level; the blocking force is directed to the left.

51. Look to the right and bring both fists down to the left side, the right in front of the left.

Application of a Left Inside-Snapping Block
(see Fig. 49 opposite page)

1. As the opponent begins a right front-snap kick to your groin, snap the left foot up off the floor.

2. (49) Block the opponent's kick with the bottom of the left foot.

52. Strike to the right with both fists simultaneously. As both fists continue to the right, the arms are parallel to the floor and the left is directly in front of the chest.

53. Upon completion of the strike, both arms are at shoulder level. *Note:* Both fists must start and stop at the same time.

54. Bring the right foot back to the left, returning to a formal stance.

Application of a Left Fore-Fist Strike to the Nose
(see Fig. 53 opposite page)

1. As the opponent steps forward punching with his left, swing both fists to the right to meet his attack.

2. (53) Grab the opponent by the back of the neck with your right hand and pull him forward into a left fore-fist strike to the nose. *Note:* The opponent's attacking arm, the left, is made to slip under your right armpit by leaning slightly forward.

Close-up of the technique in Fig. 2.

Depths of Karate Movements

Many people associate the art of karate with violence, yet, in the true sense of the word, it is nonviolent. It is strictly an art, the same as painting, music, or jade carving. It is something beautiful to see, to study, to enjoy, and to appreciate. As much as a musician enjoys a piece of music he is playing, the emotional factor being involved, he cannot duplicate what he is playing within the same mood-range again. If he is sad or sentimental, the music will coincide with the mood.

Thus in the execution of a *kata,* the karate practitioner alone can understand exactly what is happening and what he is accomplishing. His emotions at the time may be very happy, full of joy. Fifteen minutes later, emotions being what they are, his mood may change, thus the mood of the kata is not the same and it may not be free flowing. Because of this no two can look the same, just as two handwritings are not alike.

Circle. Any movement made by man or beast is done in a circular manner. It is impossible to perform any movement in an angular manner. A cup brought to the mouth in drinking coffee, for example, forms an arc. Combing one's hair, again, is performed in an arc. Any movement made by an individual, he will find, forms a circle or part of one. Nature did not intend for man to move like robot. And, so it is with karate techniques.

Any technique performed in karate will reveal a circle or a part thereof. In punching, the fist performs a circular motion before contact. In kicking, the leg lashes out in an arc. In an upper block, the arm performs an arc from the waist to the forehead; simultaneously the fist performs its circle.

II

I

Sphere. Standing with both feet together, arms fully extended to the left and right at shoulder level, one can draw a circle from the head to the fingertips of one hand on down to the feet and up to the fingertips of the opposite hand and back up to the head (Fig. I). In doing so one will have a circle or, utilizing a third dimension, a sphere.

Standing with both feet together, arms fully extended to the front at shoulder level, one can draw a half-circle from the head to the fingertips of both hands on down to the feet (Fig. II).

IV

III

Absorption or Rejection. An attack is either absorbed or rejected within this circle, or sphere. The absorption of an attack is accomplished by bringing your opponent within this sphere, such as grabbing him and pulling him toward you, or by stepping forward and taking your sphere to the opponent (Figs. III and IV).

The rejection of an attack is accomplished by giving ground and keeping the opponent out of the sphere and at a safe distance, while striking or kicking him or blocking his attacks (Figs. V and VI).

V

VI

Conclusion

My opinion of karate in the United States is that it will be strong and hold its own as long as schools stay apart and remain independent. History proves again and again that any organization, such as a government, a business, or a club which expands and grows, takes in a large income but causes nothing but internal decay. The few in power of such groups eventually become corrupt. This is the nature of man, proved from the beginning of time itself.

In the United States there are individuals who use karate for their self-interest. An instructor will tell his students that karate is for self-defense only. Over a period of time that same instructor will enter the same student in a competition and tell him to forget all he has been told, and attack to win. This type of instructor is hypocritical in his teaching, for karate is an art—not a sport. Competitions are held only for the name of the school. If a student wins, his name is forgotten but the name of the school is enhanced.

Karate is an art and has been since its origin, kept so by the great masters of the past. Who is bold enough to step forward and say that the masters were wrong and he is right? Only he who has been improperly taught and who wishes to make a name for himself at the sacrifice of injury to his students and, mostly, to the art of karate.

The only true competition a man has in life is with himself. This philosophy is not my own but one which has been passed down to me, and I think it is the most honest philosophy of karate.

My sincerest thanks are extended to karate masters Edward Unsen and George I. Yamamoto for their patience, understanding, and continual teaching along this line of thought. I pray that I may continue to convey this thought to any and all of my students.

Peter Ventresca

Index